For my parents – *J.B.*
For Catharine and Katie – *R.B.*

First published in 1988 by Hutchinson Children's Books
An imprint of Century Hutchinson Ltd
Brookmount House, 62-65 Chandos Place, Covent Garden
London WC2N 4NW

Century Hutchinson Australia Pty Ltd
16-22 Church Street, Hawthorn, Melbourne, Victoria 3122

Century Hutchinson New Zealand Limited
32-34 View Road, PO Box 40-086, Glenfield, Auckland 10

Century Hutchinson South Africa (Pty) Ltd
PO Box 337, Bergvlei 2012, South Africa

Printed and bound in Hong Kong

ISBN 0 09 173590 4

THE CHOOSING DAY

by Jennifer Beck
illustrated by Robyn Belton

HUTCHINSON

It was Briar's birthday.

In Briar's family, when it is someone's birthday
that person can choose what they want to do
all day long.

For Briar, it was like being a princess for a day.

She chose bananas and icecream for her breakfast. She ate her breakfast in her mother and father's great big bed.

She had her bath so deep and bubbly
she could barely breathe
without it frothing and foaming over the top.

'What would you like to wear today?' her mother asked.
Briar looked at her clothes in the wardrobe
then opened her box of dressing-up clothes.

She chose her favourite hat
and her favourite dress
and her favourite silver shoes.

'What are *you* going to wear?' Briar asked her mother.
'I'm not sure,' her mother replied.

'Could I choose for you?' asked Briar.

She searched through the clothes in her mother's wardrobe.
Right at the back she found a long silky dress
with frills and ribbons and a twirly swirly skirt.
There was a wispy hat that went with it.

'Please wear this dress today, Mum,' Briar pleaded.
'I've never seen you wear it, except in the photograph.'

Briar's mother was quiet for a moment.
Then she smiled at her daughter and said
with a twinkle in her eyes 'I will.'

Briar watched with delight as her mother put on
her wedding dress
and her wedding hat
and her high-heeled wedding shoes.

Very soon Briar and her mother were dressed
and ready to go out.
They were going to the shops to choose
special treats for the birthday tea.

As they waited at the bus stop, Briar said
'People will know when they see us
that today is a special day.
I wonder what they will say?'

But when they got on the bus
the driver just stared at them
and said 'Er ... um ... Where to?'

And the passengers in the bus
looked at Briar and her mother
and looked at one another
and said nothing.

And when they went into the butcher's shop
to buy little red sausages for the birthday tea
the butcher just stared at them
and said 'Er ... um ... How many?'

And the customers in the butcher's shop
looked at Briar and her mother
and looked at one another and said nothing.

And when they went into the supermarket
to buy some animal biscuits and some potato crisps
and a big piece of Briar's favourite
rainbow sponge cake
the strangers in the supermarket
looked at Briar and her mother
and looked at one another and said nothing.

And the girl at the supermarket check-out
just stared at them and said 'Er ... um ...'
and handed them the bill.

When they had finished the shopping
Briar asked her mother if they could walk home.

As they passed the school
where Briar was to start the next day
they met a group of children coming out of the gate.
They knew the teacher and some of the children.
Among them were the three friends
Briar had invited to her birthday tea.

When the children saw Briar and her mother
someone said 'They're wearing special clothes.
It must be a special day.'
'It's Briar's birthday,' explained one of her friends.

'Where are you going?' Briar asked.
'To the park for a picnic,' the children replied.
'Would you like to come too?' the teacher asked.
'Yes please!' said Briar.

So Briar and her mother
walked with the children and the teacher
to the park with the big trees
and all the different things to play on.

They slid down the slide.
They swung high on the swings.
They spun around on the round-about
and bounced up and down on the see-saw.

Briar climbed a tree with one of her friends.
Her mother danced Ring-a-ring-a-rosy on the spring grass
and twirled and swirled her long white skirt.

Just then, Briar saw someone special arrive.
It was her father.

'Hullo,' he said with a grin.
'You look as if you're having fun.
I'm on my way home for lunch.
I've bought the lemonade for the party tea.'

'Let's have the party now!' exclaimed Briar.
'Please can you stay?'

Briar's father looked from his daughter
to his wife, and smiled.
'I will,' he replied, 'although I'm not
properly dressed for the occasion.'

What a party they had.

They all shared the red sausages
and the animal biscuits and the potato crisps.
They all shared the children's sandwiches
and cookies and fruit.

Briar's father used his silver pocket knife
to cut the rainbow sponge birthday cake
into enough pieces for everyone.

Afterwards, they all had a drink of cool fizzy lemonade.

Then the teacher glanced at her watch.
It was time for the children to go back to school.
'Thanks for the party!' said Briar's new classmates.
'See you tomorrow,' smiled the teacher.

'Would our princess and our queen
like a ride home in my coach?' asked Briar's father.
'Oh yes!' Briar replied. 'But just for once ...

... could we ride on the back?'